Clever COGZ
THE BOOK OF
DIGGERS & DOZERS

By Neil Clark

Quarto is the authority on a wide range of topics.

Quarto educates, entertains and enriches the lives of
our readers—enthusiasts and lovers of hands-on living.

www.quartoknows.com

Author & illustrator: Neil Clark
Consultant: Pete Robinson
Editor: Harriet Stone
Designer: Sarah Chapman-Suire
Editorial Director: Laura Knowles
Creative Director: Malena Stojic

© 2019 Quarto Publishing plc

This edition first published in 2019
by QEB Publishing,
an imprint of The Quarto Group.
26391 Crown Valley Parkway, Suite 220
Mission Viejo, CA 92691, USA
T: +1 949 380 7510
F: +1 949 380 7575
www.QuartoKnows.com

A CIP record for this book is available from
the Library of Congress.

ISBN 978 0 7112 4341 5

Manufactured in Shenzhen, China PP092019

9 8 7 6 5 4 3 2 1

Hello, I'm Clever Cogz!
Follow me and my sidekicks, Nutty & Bolt, to learn about diggers, bulldozers, and other working machines.

CONTENTS

Working Machines

Working machines like diggers and dozers are used to help people do tough jobs. These earth-crunching vehicles are perfect for digging, lifting, and flattening. There are lots of different types. Let's take a look!

Excavator

Excavators are the most well-known diggers around. Learn about them on page 12.

These muddy machines are so exciting!

Tractor

VROOM! VROOM! Tractors can make a tough job easy! Learn about tractors on page 10.

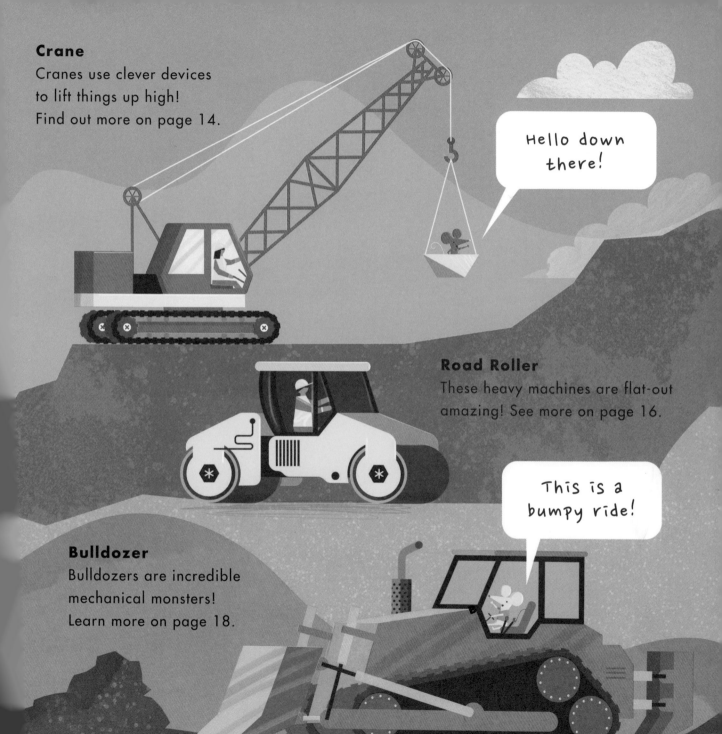

Crane
Cranes use clever devices to lift things up high! Find out more on page 14.

Hello down there!

Road Roller
These heavy machines are flat-out amazing! See more on page 16.

This is a bumpy ride!

Bulldozer
Bulldozers are incredible mechanical monsters! Learn more on page 18.

Backhoe Loader

READY, STEADY, RUMBLE! Diggers are big, powerful, and noisy. This digger is called a backhoe loader. You can usually find them working on building sites. Have you ever seen one?

The driver sits in the **cab**. The driver's seat spins around so the driver can face the front or the back.

This giant scoop is a **front loader**. It can lift 8,800 pounds (4000 kg).

Unlike the one on a car, a digger's **exhaust pipe** sticks up in the air so it doesn't get damaged by the bumpy ground.

wow, that's like lifting three cars!

A digger is so big you need **steps** to climb inside!

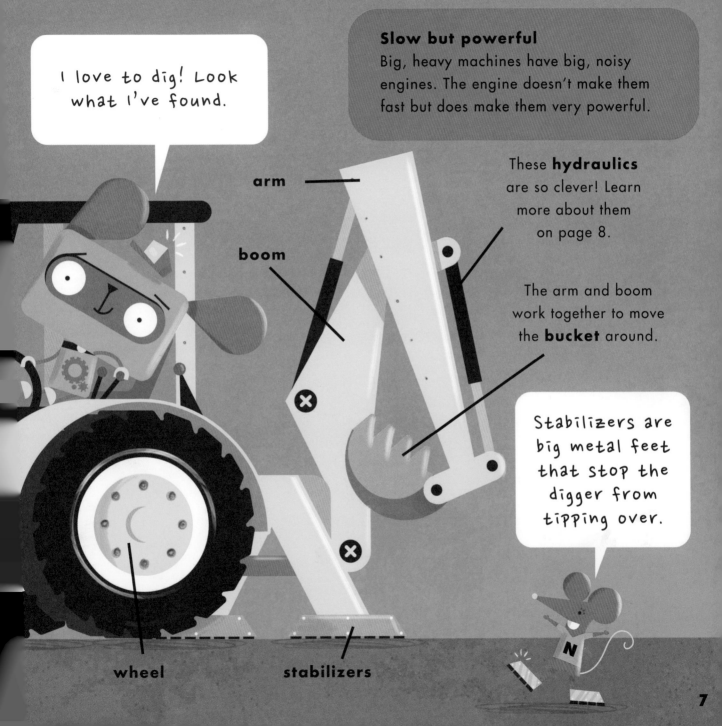

I love to dig! Look what I've found.

Slow but powerful
Big, heavy machines have big, noisy engines. The engine doesn't make them fast but does make them very powerful.

arm

boom

These **hydraulics** are so clever! Learn more about them on page 8.

The arm and boom work together to move the **bucket** around.

Stabilizers are big metal feet that stop the digger from tipping over.

wheel

stabilizers

Hydraulics

Many big machines use hydraulics. The hydraulics on a digger are like the muscles in your arms! They're what give the digger its digging power. Let's see how they work.

Nutty's little weight is able to push up my bigger weight using hydraulics.

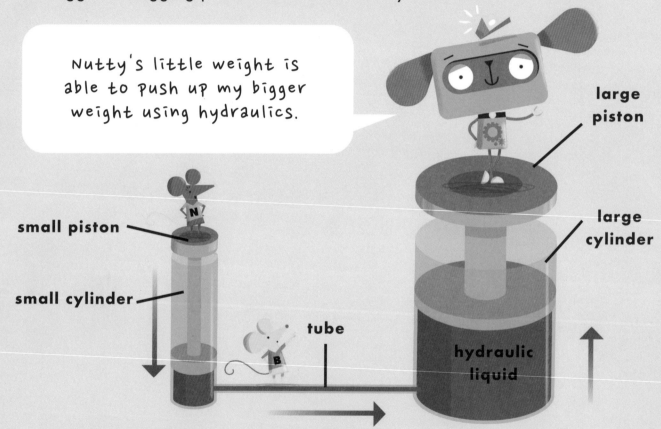

large piston

large cylinder

small piston

small cylinder

tube

hydraulic liquid

Under Pressure

Pressure is when something gets squeezed. Nutty is pushing down on the small piston that she is standing on. The liquid in the small piston is being pushed downward and squeezed along the thin tube. This creates pressure. The pressure pushes the liquid up into the large cylinder, which pushes Cogz and the large piston upward!

How digger hydraulics work

1) The pump pushes the liquid along a thin tube.

2) The liquid is squeezed into the cylinder.

3) The pressure pushes the piston forward inside the cylinder.

4) The digger's arm moves up.

pump

water fight!

Water Pressure
Have you ever squirted a water pistol? Pushing the trigger creates pressure which squeezes the water out of the pistol. Hydraulics work in a similar way.

Tractor

CHUG CHUG CHUG! It's a tractor! These vehicles can be used to do lots of different jobs. Farmers use them for plowing fields, pulling trailers, and planting crops.

I'm using this tractor to make holes so we can plant lots of trees!

Watch out, there's a tractor nearby! Tractors use a flashing **warning light** to warn people they are coming.

exhaust pipe

cab

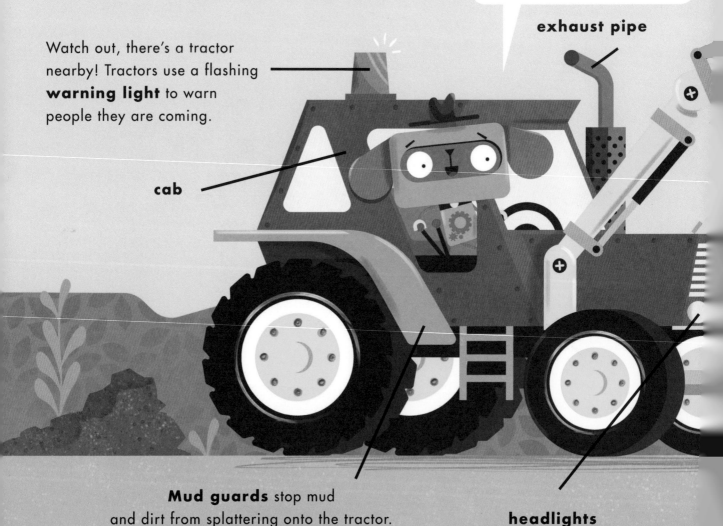

Mud guards stop mud and dirt from splattering onto the tractor.

headlights

Attachments

Tractors can have different tools, called attachments, to do different jobs. The one Cogz is using is called a hole digger. It is shaped like a giant screw. As it spins, it lifts the soil to make a hole.

Tree-mendous!

Wheels

Tractors and diggers have big back wheels and smaller front wheels. The big wheels have chunky grips. This helps the tractor drive across muddy ground. Small front wheels make it easier to turn tight corners.

Hello? I think I'm stuck down here!

Excavator

What scoops, grabs, swivels, and digs? That's right, an excavator. Excavators are used for digging big holes and moving earth. They can also be used for knocking down buildings.

Tracks

Most excavators have metal tracks, sometimes called caterpillar tracks. Having tracks instead of wheels means that the excavator can easily move over bumpy and muddy land.

Sprockets

The metal tracks wrap around strange-looking cogs, called sprockets. The engine turns the sprockets, which turn the tracks and the excavator moves along.

That's a lot of clever cogs!

engine

fuel tank

tracks

sprocket

Slow Mover

Excavators may be fast at digging, but they're very slow at moving around. With a top speed of 6 miles (9 km) per hour, this one will need a lift on the back of a truck to get to its next job.

Diesel vs. Electric

Most big machines are fueled by diesel. Burning diesel creates smelly fumes that are bad for the environment. There are new, electric powered excavators that will help keep our planet clean.

boom

The bucket has an extra part called a **thumb**. It turns the bucket into a giant claw, perfect for grabbing things.

arm

Thumbs up!

bucket

An army tank also uses tracks to move.

Crane

It's time to learn about cranes! These machines reach high into the air. Their height and power are used to lift heavy objects. Some things are so heavy that a crane is the only machine that can move them.

A crane's **boom** reaches way up into the sky!

Cranes have been used for thousands of years. The ancient Egyptians used them to move water.

The **main body** can spin all the way around.

The **counterweight** is made from solid concrete or steel. It stops the crane from falling forward.

tracks

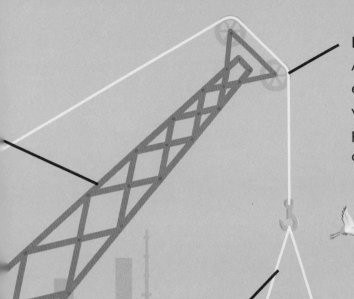

Pulleys

A pulley is a simple machine that makes it easier to lift things. It is made from rope that wraps around a wheel. When the rope is pulled down on one end, it lifts the load up on the other end.

The biggest mobile crane is over 800 feet (245 m) high.

That's as tall as 50 giraffes standing on top of each other!

This special **wire rope** is made from steel, which makes it very strong.

The **load** is the objects that the crane lifts up.

Cranes are named after the crane bird. They have a long neck and long legs.

Road Roller

Roll up, roll up! This heavyweight is spectacular to see. A road roller is a vehicle used to flatten and squash the ground. The roads we drive on are nice and smooth thanks to these machines.

Road rollers can flatten soil, gravel, concrete, or even rocks. Rock and roll!

I'd better stay out of its way! Eek!

rolling drum

Roller History

1800 – The first road rollers were
pulled along by horses.

1865 – British engineers
Aveling and Porter invented
the steamroller.

1950 – Diesel-powered rollers became
more popular than steamrollers.

2020 – New road rollers are powered by electricity.

Don't worry, Nutty.
Road rollers can
only go at 4 miles
(6 km) per hour.

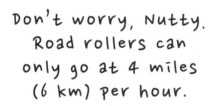

*The biggest rollers
weigh up to 22 tons.
That's the same as 15 cars!*

Bulldozer

Watch out! A bulldozer will crush and push anything in its path. They are used for moving materials like soil, sand, or rubble. Bulldozers can be found at building sites, mines, quarries, and on farms.

Safety First!

Bulldozers are great at knocking down things such as buildings or trees. This can be dangerous work.

That's why I've got my hard hat on.

The **ripper** is a giant claw that rips into the ground. It breaks up any big lumps of land that need to be moved.

These tracks are called **high tracks**. They help the bulldozer move over muddy ground.

A bulldozer can weigh 110 tons. That's the same as 100 bulls!

Amazing Blades

The blade is a giant wedge of metal that does all the pushing. It is the most important part of a bulldozer. The blade can move up, down, forward, and backward. It can even tilt left and right. The bottom edge of the blade is very sharp.

blade

Armored Bulldozers

Bulldozers are used by the army to clear battlefields and to build shelters. This one is covered in armor to protect it from explosions.

Giants!

This is the Bagger 293. It's the biggest digger in the world. This type of digger is called a bucket wheel excavator, or BWE. It works at a coal mine and digs 240,000 tons of coal a day.

wire ropes

> wow! This digger is so big that it needs five people to control it. Nutty and Bolt are helping out. Can you spot them?

The coal falls out the buckets onto a **conveyor belt**. This carries the coal to be loaded onto trains.

This BWE needs 17 megawatts of electricity to keep going. That's enough to power a whole town!

Nine sets of **tracks** hold the digger's weight. It can only move very slowly.

Coal Power

When coal is burned it releases lots of energy. We use it to make electricity that powers our homes. But burning coal gives off gases that harm our planet. There are other ways of creating electricty that don't harm our planet, such as wind and solar power.

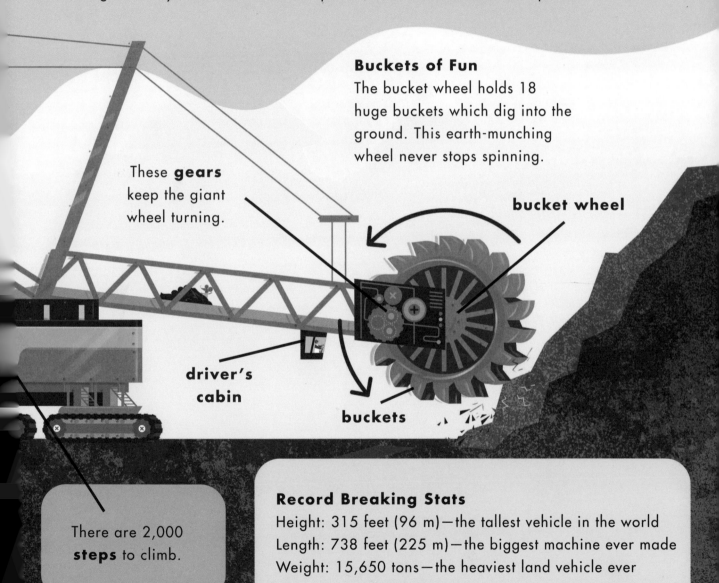

Buckets of Fun

The bucket wheel holds 18 huge buckets which dig into the ground. This earth-munching wheel never stops spinning.

bucket wheel

These **gears** keep the giant wheel turning.

driver's cabin

buckets

There are 2,000 **steps** to climb.

Record Breaking Stats

Height: 315 feet (96 m)—the tallest vehicle in the world
Length: 738 feet (225 m)—the biggest machine ever made
Weight: 15,650 tons—the heaviest land vehicle ever

Robot Diggers

There are some diggers that work without a driver inside. Clever computers and reliable robots are taking control.

Look, I can be a robot digger.

Remote Control

How can a machine be controlled by someone who is far away? A person uses buttons and levers to send signals to a machine. Inside the machine, a receiver picks up the signals and tells the vehicle what to do.

Just like my toy car!

signal

receiver inside

controller

Sensors

This is a self-driving digger. It works by using a clever box of sensors on its roof. Its computer remembers where to go and what to do. This technology is also used in driverless cars.

Demolition Bot

The Brokk 800 uses a big hammer to smash up chunks of concrete. This work can be dangerous. It's much safer for a robot excavator to do it.

XE15R

This is a remote-controlled hydraulic digger. It's only about 3 feet (1 m) wide but can be controlled from over 330 feet (100 m) away. It may be small, but it's very smart.

Small and smart, just like me!

I hope you've enjoyed learning about diggers and dozers. Now let's test our knowledge.

Nutty and Bolt have come up with six questions. It's time to start digging for answers!

1. Which machine uses a blade and a ripper?

2. What are the metal tracks on a digger called?

3. Which technology squeezes liquids through tubes to make things move?

4. What clever device do cranes use to lift heavy objects?

5. What kind of digger is the Bagger 293?

6. Which animals powered the first road rollers?

Answers

1. A bulldozer, 2. Caterpillar tracks, 3. Hydraulics, 4. Pulleys, 5. A bucket wheel excavator (BWE), 6. Horses